MEXICO: THE GEOGRAPHY

SOUTH OF THE BORDER

Laura Conlon

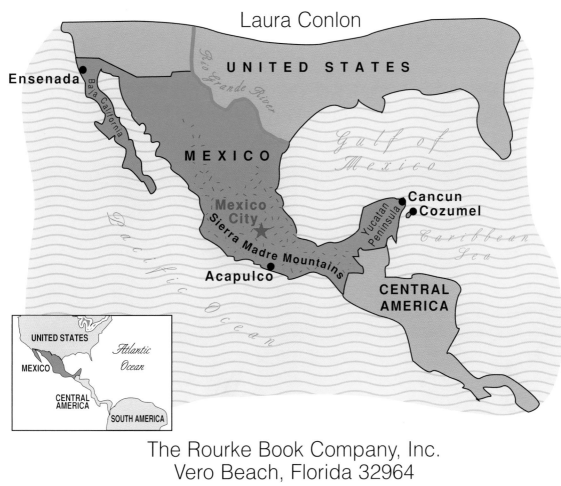

The Rourke Book Company, Inc.
Vero Beach, Florida 32964

Edited by Sandra A. Robinson

PHOTO CREDITS
© Frank Balthis: cover, pages 8, 12; © Steve Bentsen: pages 4, 10;
© Steve Warble: page 15; © Robert Pelham: page 17;
© Jerry Hennen: page 18; © Lynn Stone: page 21;
courtesy Mexico's Ministry of Tourism: title page, pages 7, 13

Library of Congress Cataloging-in-Publication Data

Conlon, Laura, 1959-
    Mexico: the geography / Laura Conlon.
    p. cm. — (South of the border)
    Includes index.
    ISBN 1-55916-056-X
    1. Mexico—Description and travel—Juvenile literature.
[1. Mexico—Description and travel.] I. Title. II. Series.
F1216.5.C66   1994
917.204'835—dc20   94-15000
                                                       CIP
                                                       AC
Printed in the USA

TABLE OF CONTENTS

MEXICO: THE GEOGRAPHY

Visitors to Mexico are always surprised. First-time visitors from America are especially surprised. Why? They expect all of Mexico to be hot, dry and brushy, like parts of Texas, New Mexico and Arizona.

However, Mexico is a North American country with 31 different states. Two-thirds of Mexico is covered by mountains and high **plateaus. Tropical rain forests,** deserts, seashores and green valleys are also part of Mexico's landscape.

Part of Mexico is covered by dense, green rain forest

MOUNTAINS

Three mountain ranges stand tall in Mexico. They are all part of the Sierra Madre Mountains.

The mountainous areas of Mexico are extremely rugged. Some **canyons** are deeper than parts of the Grand Canyon. Many of these **remote,** or hard-to-reach, areas have never been explored.

Mexico has several mountain **volcanoes.** Mount Orizaba is an extinct — or inactive — volcano. Reaching 18,700 feet, it is Mexico's highest peak. The last volcano to **erupt** in Mexico was Mount Chinchon in 1982.

Rugged mountains rise above Copper Canyon in the Mexican state of Chihuahua

PLATEAUS

An enormous plateau called the *altiplano* lies between Mexico's eastern and western mountain ranges. Much of the northern part of the altiplano is desert. This area has little rainfall and hot daytime temperatures.

The southern part of the altiplano is the Central Plateau. Temperatures here are cooler, and more rainfall makes farming possible. Most Mexican people live in the large cities on the Central Plateau.

Most of Mexico's people live on the flat plateaus

FORESTS

Pine forests cling to mountain slopes in central Mexico. "Forests" of thorny bushes cover some desert areas.

The most amazing forests in Mexico are the tropical rain forests. These are thick, wet forests that are always green. They are home to many plants and animals, including monkeys, jaguars and scarlet macaws.

One rain forest is called the Quintana Roo. **Chicle** is taken from sapodilla trees in the forest. Chicle is used to make chewing gum.

Tiny huts peep out of clearings in the rain forests of Tamaulipas, Mexico

Sand ripples across dunes on Mexico's Baja Peninsula

Rocks and palm trees line the beach at Tulum

COASTLINES

Sandy beaches line much of Mexico's seacoast and its sea islands. In other places, the shores have rocks and cliffs.

The two coasts — Atlantic and Pacific — nearly join at the Isthmus of Tehuantepec. This **isthmus** is only 130 miles across.

Because the water is warm and clear, sea life is plentiful. **Coral reefs** are hiding places for hundreds of kinds of colorful fish and other sea creatures.

Some of Mexico's more than 6,000 miles of shoreline are sandy

PENINSULAS

A **peninsula** is a long strip of land almost surrounded by water. Mexico has two special peninsulas.

The Baja Peninsula on the west coast is 800 miles long. It is one of the longest peninsulas in the world.

The Yucatan Peninsula in eastern Mexico has no rivers on its surface. Instead, its rivers run underground. Large holes called *cenotes* on the Yucatan surface lead to the underground rivers.

A lighted stairway (right) leads to a cenote on the Yucatan Peninsula

RIVERS AND LAKES

The Rio Grande is Mexico's longest river. It forms about 1,300 miles of Mexico's border with the United States.

The largest lake in Mexico is Lake Chapala. It covers 417 square miles.

Lake Xochimilco is famous for its floating gardens. Long ago, people created small islands in this lake by heaping mud onto piles of twigs. Then they planted flowers and vegetables in the mud. These beautiful gardens still float on the lake today.

The Rio Grande forms about 1,300 miles of the border between Mexico and the United States

DESERTS

Northwestern Mexico is rugged desert. Much of it is a roadless wilderness.

Rocky mountains rise above canyons and craters. The Grand Desert is a sea of sand that flows with the wind.

The Sonoran Desert is a more lively desert. It is the home of great, treelike saguaro cactus that are more than 50 feet tall. Badgers, coyotes, bobcats, lizards, snakes, scorpions and flocks of birds live among the desert plants.

The Sonoran Desert blooms each spring in Sonora, Mexico

CLIMATE

Climate is the kind of weather that a place has over a long period of time. Mexico covers 761,604 square miles. Because it is a large country, the climate changes from place to place.

Mexico's Gulf Coast, for example, is warm throughout the year. It has heavy rainfall at times.

The deserts are dry and very hot during the summer months.

Mexico's mountains are always cool at 8,000 feet above sea level. The highest mountain peaks are *cold!* The peaks have snow all year.

Glossary

canyon (KAN yun) — a long, narrow valley between high cliffs

chicle (CHEEK lay) — sap from the sapodilla tree, which is used in making chewing gum

coral reef (KOR uhl REEF) — an undersea platform of rock built over a long period of time by coral animals

erupt (eh RUPT) — to burst out

isthmus (IS mus) — a narrow strip of land with water on each side

peninsula (pen IN soo la) — a land area almost entirely surrounded by water

plateau (pla TOE) — an area of flat land that is higher than the land around it

remote (re MOTE) — far away or out-of-the-way

tropical rain forest (TROP i kul RANE FOR est) — a thick, always-green forest in a tropical area that has much rain

volcano (vol KAY no) — an opening in the Earth's crust through which lava, rocks and ashes erupt

INDEX